Little People, BIG DREAMS®
RIHANNA

Written by
Maria Isabel Sánchez Vegara

Illustrated by
Niña Mata

Frances Lincoln
Children's Books

On the sunny island of Barbados, surrounded by the sound of waves and calypso music, there lived a little girl called Robyn. But it was with her middle name, Rihanna, that she would one day become a superstar.

Her dad wasn't around much, so Rihanna often had to look after her two brothers while her mum was at work. To keep them smiling, she sang and danced around the house, turning the living room into their own little stage.

School wasn't always easy. Some kids teased Rihanna because her skin was lighter than theirs. But she didn't let their words dim her sparkle. Instead, she started a band with some friends and turned up the volume on her dreams.

Rihanna and her friends were still thinking of a name for their band when they got the chance to perform for an American musician visiting Barbados. He was amazed by Rihanna's powerful voice and vibrant energy.

Soon after, Rihanna was invited to an audition in New York City, far away from her tiny island. She felt nervous, but she sang her heart out for the head of a big music company. Her performance earned her a record deal that same day!

At seventeen, Rihanna burst on to the music scene with a hit, 'Pon de Replay'. The title means 'play it again' in Bajan Creole, her home language. The beat was so catchy, it had everyone dancing, making Rihanna a star almost overnight!

Two years later, Rihanna surprised everyone with an edgy short haircut and a new, bold style. She released 'Umbrella', an amazing hit about friends helping each other. Thanks to that song, she won her first Grammy music award.

But all that success didn't come easy. Behind the bright lights were sleepless nights, long hours in the studio and endless travelling. Rihanna didn't do it for fame or money – she did it because she truly loved music.

Despite years at the top, Rihanna continued to push herself. 'Diamonds' wasn't just another hit – it was an anthem about strength and self-belief. The song touched people all over the world, inspiring them to shine in their own way.

But Rihanna wanted to help people shine in real life, too. She started a charity named after her grandparents, Clara and Lionel. For years, she held a big party called the Diamond Ball to raise money for those who need it most.

Her love for colour, style and fairness sparked a big idea. She created a make-up and clothing brand with shades for every skin tone and sizes for every body. She was also the first Black woman to lead a fashion label for a famous luxury company.

While expecting her babies, Rihanna wore sparkly tops and sheer dresses – showing off her bump instead of hiding it. She helped people see that a growing belly is something to celebrate, inspiring mothers to feel confident and proud.

With every step she took, Rihanna – the little girl from Barbados – proved that we all have a diamond inside us, ready to shine bright. All we have to do is look within and see the beauty that was always there.

RIHANNA

(Born 1988)

2005

2007

Robyn Rihanna Fenty was born on the Caribbean island of Barbados. Her dad had a lot of problems and her childhood wasn't easy. Singing and listening to music became her escape. Aged fifteen, she got a lucky break – the chance to audition for an American record producer, Evan Rogers, who was visiting the island. He helped her record her first ever song. In the summer of 2005, the seventeen-year-old found herself in New York City, singing in front of legendary rapper Jay-Z, head of the Def Jam Recordings record label. He signed her there and then. Her first two albums did well, but she really became a superstar in 2007, when she changed her style for something edgier. Her song 'Umbrella' became one of the year's biggest anthems. Three years later, she became the only female artist in

2023

2025

history to have four Number 1 singles on the US Billboard charts in a single year. In 2012, Rihanna set up the Clara Lionel Foundation, which works with communities to improve education, healthcare and more. In her late twenties, she took a break from music and turned her talents to business. Fenty Beauty, her make-up brand, was the first to include foundation for dozens of different skin shades. Her clothing line, Savage X Fenty, celebrated women of all shapes and sizes. Rihanna wanted everyone to feel included. In 2023, she made a comeback to the stage at the Super Bowl Halftime show. Her iconic performance revealed a proud baby bump – a second child with rapper A$AP Rocky. One of the bestselling artists of all time, Rihanna is known around the world as a style icon and queen of pop.

Want to find out more about **Rihanna**?

Have a read of this great book:

Rihanna: A Little Golden Book Biography by Regina Andreoni

Text © 2026 Maria Isabel Sánchez Vegara. Illustrations © 2026 Niña Mata.
Original idea of the series by Maria Isabel Sánchez Vegara, published by Alba Editorial, s.l.u.
"Little People, BIG DREAMS" and "Pequeña & Grande" are trademarks of
Alba Editorial s.l.u. and/or Beautifool Couple S.L.
First published in the UK in 2026 by Frances Lincoln Children's Books, an imprint of The Quarto Group.
1 Triptych Place, London, SE1 9SH, United Kingdom. T 020 7700 6700 www.Quarto.com
EEA Representation, WTS Tax d.o.o., Žanova ulica 3, 4000 Kranj, Slovenia. www.wts-tax.si

All rights reserved.
No part of this publication may be reproduced, stored in a retrieval system, or transmitted, in any form,
or by any means, electrical, mechanical, photocopying, recording or otherwise without the prior written
permission of the publisher or a licence permitting restricted copying.

This book is not authorised, licensed or approved by Rihanna.
Any faults are the publisher's who will be happy to rectify for future printings.
A catalogue record for this book is available from the British Library.
ISBN 978-1-80570-174-3
Set in Futura BT.

Published by Juliet Matthews · Edited by Claire Saunders
Designed by Sasha Moxon and Izzy Bowman
Production by Robin Boothroyd
Manufactured in Shanghai, China CC112025
1 3 5 7 9 8 6 4 2

Photographic acknowledgements (pages 28–29, from left to right): 1. Rihanna before the start of the 2005 US Open at the USTA National Tennis Center in Flushing Meadows Corona Park, New York City, on 27th August, 2005 © Bryan Bedder/Getty Images. 2. Rihanna performs in Tokyo, Japan, for the Live Earth series of concerts, on 7th July, 2007 © Koji Watanabe/Getty Images. 3. Rihanna performs during the Apple Music Super Bowl LVII Halftime Show at State Farm Stadium in Glendale, Arizona, on 12th February, 2023 © Kevin Mazur/Getty Images for Roc Nation. 4. Rihanna at the 78th annual Cannes Film Festival at Palais des Festivals in Cannes, France, on May 19, 2025 © Karwai Tang/WireImage.

Scan the QR code for free activity sheets, teachers' notes and more information about the series at www.littlepeoplebigdreams.com